Learning Wordpress

A comprehensive step-by-step guide to building a
high-quality business website using Wordpress.

by

William Shane Roberson

Learning Wordpress

Special Thanks

This book would simply not be possible if it were not for the love and support of Jesus Christ, my lord and savior! Second, my amazing family, who put up with my daydreaming and idea dribbling (bouncing ideas off them). Special thanks to my wife Tanya, my sons Chase and Chance, and my wonderful mother-in-law Celia Escobar. You guys are my heart and I love you all!

Preface

This book is a nod to all of the entrepreneurs and startups (small businesses) out there that are going after their dreams. Our entrepreneurs and startups are the heart and soul of this great country. According to the U.S. Small Business Association (SBA), the 28 million small businesses in America account for 54 percent of all U.S. sales. In addition, small businesses provide 55 percent of all jobs and

66 percent of all the new jobs since the 1970s. Let that sink in for a moment.

We live in the greatest country in the world that allows everyone in it an opportunity to go after their dreams. To be clear, it is never easy, and nothing is promised, but if you work hard enough and are lucky enough, you can turn your small business into a big business. I created a short formula that I often share with entrepreneurs and clients: **D + F = O**. It translates to **D**rive + **F**ocus = **O**pportunity. If you work hard and stay focused on your goals, you will create opportunity. Keep in mind that opportunity is not a promise nor a guarantee. Actually, the word "opportunity" is defined as "a set of circumstances that make it possible to do something." In America, that is more than enough!

What Is It And Who Is It For?

The purpose of this book is to offer a comprehensive tutorial on setting up, designing and maintaining a **high-quality**

Wordpress website for your business, idea, product or service. This book is for anyone who does not have the budget for a reputable digital marketing agency and requires that ever-important Internet presence. Though I will refer to "your business," this book can help anyone who wants to build a Wordpress website. This book provides the tools you need to build a high-quality website for nearly any industry or service with hardly any costs. It will also allow you to bypass some of the less than helpful professionals and common mistakes people make by poorly investing in "design and development." We will discuss the different professionals In the next chapter.

PLEASE NOTE: This book is **not** the last step in your business growth. Your website is only the beginning of becoming a profitable online business. If you care enough to build your website, then you will care enough to begin planning to partner with a reputable digital marketing agency. In this book I will show you how to build a fully functioning website using tools, tips and shortcuts the professionals use. However, please understand that no website will be a customer-generating machine until it is properly marketed, a clear customer avatar is defined, and a sales funnel is created for them. These high-level online marketing strategies are beyond the scope of this book, but let it be known, **a website is only a small part of your online business** and its success. In short, I always recommend partnering with a reputable digital marketing agency, preferably in your local area. If you do choose a digital marketing agency that is not local to you, be sure that it is reputable and well known. If you have no digital marketing agencies near you, then you can contact me directly at shane@integritywebstudios.com to see if my agency would be a good fit for you, your company and your goals. We would love to help you create your success story.

Tutorial Overload

There are a lot of helpful tutorials out there today. However, I found that many of them are too narrow in scope, which leaves you searching for the next step in yet another tutorial

— or worse, cobbling together a website that looks and functions like a child threw it together. There are many great tutorials out there, but stumbling through a virtual endless field of them to find your next step via trial and error is simply not efficient enough for me or you. I wanted to create something that I could put in the hands of people to help guide them through a **high-quality** Wordpress website build specifically geared toward growing the business or brand efficiently. In short, my goal is to shorten your path from Wordpress newbie to revenue-generating website builder!

Wordpress Evolution

One thing to keep in mind before we dive in is that Wordpress is constantly and consistently evolving. Most changes through Wordpress updates are incremental at best and seldom change the overall design and functionality at any given time. However, please consider that the Wordpress version available during the writing of this book may have some functionality or design changes that are slightly different in future releases. During the writing of this book, Wordpress released a few updates, moving from version 4.7.5 to version 4.8 with no major changes to functionality that would affect the descriptions in this book. Many of the Wordpress basics described here are fundamental and have not changed at all since the birth of Wordpress.

Bypassing the Professional

When I refer to "professionals," you must understand I am using the term loosely. There are different levels of web design professionals out there. Though many are capable of offering some level of expertise in the web design process, only some are qualified to fulfill the needs of your company within your budget. Ultimately, no company can be a wild success on the web without either an in-house digital marketing division or a digital marketing agency working for them. Below I will discuss a few common web designer types you may run into.

The Coffee Shop Guru

The first of these is what I call the "Coffee Shop Guru" (CSG). Though the CSG may have a fundamental understanding of the web-building process and talk a good game, this does not mean he's the guy you should pay to build your website. More people lose money to the CSG than any other professional. In my experience, the CSG loves to talk the talk but seldom does he have the experience required to offer anything more than what this book does. Though he may be the most affordable, he also is usually the first to bail on a project the second he has a problem or gets a real job. His lack of understanding and poor business skills may cost you big. I cannot tell you how many clients I have now who first lost thousands of dollars to crap projects that were either never finished or poorly executed. This does not count the potential lost revenue from an incomplete or poorly designed website. If you are considering the CSG, you'd be better off with this book because you can probably do a better job yourself.

Your Cousin's Sister Who Has a Friend Whose Son Can Do It

Unless this distant connection actually owns or works at a reputable digital marketing and design agency, do not hire this person, who is essentially the CSG with a referral. If he owns the agency, he will charge agency prices, which defeats the purpose of designing and developing it yourself: no budget. If he works at an agency, it does not mean he is a good designer/developer. (For example, simply working in a hospital does not mean a person can perform surgery.)

Web Designers

Professional Web Designers (WD) are essentially CSGs who have grown up and have more experience, better business savvy and an office. They will work full time and have some vested interest in their own brand, such as a working office and cool logos and branding. They are usually much more professional, complete with contracts to sign, processes to follow and set prices in the $3000-to-$5,000 range. They are the most reasonable alternative to building the website yourself. The only problem with web designers is that they lack a fundamental understanding of (or willingness to acknowledge) holistic marketing, and more important, driving traffic to this new website. They typically deal in commodities such as websites, codes and frameworks like Wordpress, php, Javascript and jQuery, logos, photography and so on. They are selling a specific product and do not care how it performs (whether it generates a return on investment) once it has been built. I should know because this is where I thrived for years before finally deciding to change. I was not happy delivering a product that ultimately does not solve the problem most companies have, getting new customers.

Digital Marketing Agencies

Digital Marketing Agencies (DMAs) employ older, better-educated or evolved web designers who were tired of selling a commodity that does not solve the core concern of a client (to get more business/generate a return). DMAs design for a holistic marketing process that requires extensive research on your company, product, competition, markets and other trends to address the core issue — getting more clients or customers. A website is a small cog in the engine of creating new paying customers/clients. But a website that does not generate some profit is an expense, **not** an investment.

A DMA is a must for any company as it matures — the basic website is simply not sufficient. The biggest problem with DMAs is that they are costly. Most DMAs cost between $10,000 and $50,000. Mind you, the DMA is actually delivering a positive return on your investment. However, many smaller companies simply cannot swing the upfront cost without borrowing money, which is never the best option if it can be avoided.

Skip This!

This book is meant to be used as a no-fluff guide to shorten your path to a fully functioning website that not only showcases your brand but stands as something you can be proud of. I am a firm believer in efficiency and encourage you to skip over sections of this book that are not relevant to you or that you may already know. In addition, you should save this book and use it as a quick referral guide if you need a refresher in the future.

What Is Wordpress?

If you are reading this book, then it is likely you have either heard of Wordpress, already have backend experience with a Wordpress website, or you are about to begin developing your own Wordpress website. In an attempt to be comprehensive, I will give you a quick rundown of what Wordpress is and what it is not.

What It Is

Wordpress is a scalable, open source (free) framework that utilizes a CMS (Content Management System) to create and manage websites. It is a dashboard on the website that allows easy development of pages and content, usually without the need for code. Today, websites are much more dynamic than in the past, with a lot of automation and animation. Wordpress updates its framework consistently to stay ahead of any new technology that may enhance functionality or security. What this means for the average website is that it will continue to evolve as technology and security risks do.

Wordpress was originally created specifically for blogging. A blog is a regularly updated website typically written in an informal or conversational style by an individual or small group — think digital magazine with a discussion option. Fast-forward 14 years to today (yes, you read that correctly: Wordpress is more than 14 years old — older than Facebook and Twitter) and we find an equally flexible website framework that is now developed for every industry, product and service imaginable. In addition, over the last 14 years, Wordpress has grown to become the most used framework globally, taking up nearly 30 percent market share and more than 68 different languages. This means that of all the websites on the Internet today, nearly 30 percent (27 percent as of May 2017) are running on Wordpress.

Because Wordpress is open source and shares its source code freely, developers all over the world have created new and exciting services, themes and plugins for Wordpress. This open code sharing that empowers the developers and the CMS that empowers the average user are both key factors in why Wordpress is so wildly popular globally. In summary, Wordpress is literally made so everyone can use it.

What It Is Not

Wordpress is not a static cookie-cutter template as in the old days, when websites created from the same templates would be obviously similar. Though Wordpress utilizes themes that are basically style templates, rest assured the highly customizable features, layouts and functions allow users to create very different looks and feels even if they used the same theme.

Wordpress is not for anyone needing a site in a few days. If you need a website in a week or less, this is not for you. Again, I am teaching you to create a **high-quality** website, and a novice would find it daunting to do so in a few weeks, much less in one. Yes, it is very possible, but I like to slow down newbies and clients so they focus on the quality rather than the speed of launching their websites.

Though Wordpress has a very easy to learn CMS, it still requires a bit of practice and patience to master. If you plan on having/using your high-quality website for more than a few years, then you are in the right place, learning the right tool. However, if you only require a short-term solution or you are in a rush, you may do better investing your time in a DIY website builder. Let me make it clear that I am not a fan of those types of sites, but I am a firm believer that rushing through any project, much less rushing while learning a new technology, will ultimately cost you.

CMS

Thanks to Wordpress, CMSs are now a staple of web design and development across all platforms and frameworks. CMS offers the developer an easy way to manage the pages, files, and functions of a website. The Wordpress CMS uses WYSIWYG [pronounced: ˈwizēˌwig] (What You See Is What You Get) editors without requiring the knowledge or use of code and markup. Think of your document editor: Much like Word, a WYSIWYG offers a way to add text, basic markup and images to your pages or posts without having to understand or use code to do so. This alone is extremely empowering to most online marketers who used to be forced to rely solely on developers/designers such as myself to create, add, or update their content. Using a CMS to develop a website is referred to as "Frontend Development."

Plugins

Wordpress could be awesome with the CMS alone. However, it also offers a great way to add even more functionality to your website through the use of "Plugins." A plugin is simply a specific functionality that is easily integrated with your website. There are literally tens of thousands of various plugins that cover nearly any need imaginable for a website — creating forms, adding animation, sending digital contracts to be signed online, creating and sending emails and so much more. In short, there is a plugin for every business need out there, and new plugins are being created daily. For more information on plugins, be sure to read the "Suggested Plugins" chapter of this book.

Setting Up

Before we can begin developing our website, first we need to nail down a few other elements such as hosting and email. In this chapter we will discuss how to choose a hosting company and what products you actually need from that company, then creating the environment for our new website. Finally, we will create our free email account and learn how to use it on any device. If you already have your hosting account with a cPanel, then feel free to skip to the next chapter.

Choosing a Hosting Company

A hosting company is simply a company that leases you computer space and from that makes your website live to the world via the Internet. There are many different hosting companies out there, but they are not all the same. This is why I'll take a few moments to point out some things to look for in a reputable hosting company. For starters, the larger companies such as GoDaddy, Bluehost and Inmotion Hosting are always a good start. I have my favorites, and they all have flaws but are not bad for basic affordable website hosting solutions. For premium hosting I recommend WP-Engine or Rackspace. However, you must understand that these are premium hosting companies and they charge accordingly. While they are not the most affordable options, I promise you they are worth every penny.

There are a lot more hosting companies out there, so here a few things to look for when choosing the right hosting company for your business website. One of the most important things to look for in a company is tech support availability. Ideally, you would like a hosting company with an American-based, 24/7 live tech support system in place. This is not a deal breaker, but trust me, it comes in handy. Tech supports are often outsourced overseas — not that there is anything wrong with the hosting company trying to save some money. But you do not want to have to struggle through a strong accent while talking technical Internet jargon. Next, make sure it has a 99.9 percent or better uptime. This means that the website does not go down very often. To be clear, most hosting companies do have some down time — even some of the big companies I mentioned have left my sites down for several hours — but you want as little as possible.

The last thing to look for when choosing your hosting company is that it offers a "Linux-based cPanel hosting" option. Most will have this, as it is now one of the most used out there, but just be sure before buying any hosting plan.

Domain Name

I usually recommend buying your domain name from the hosting company of choice just because it is convenient to have all of your digital assets in one place and covered by only one bill. A domain name is simply the URL, or what you type in the browser to get to your website. For example, my domain name for Integrity Web Studios is www.integritywebstudios.com. If you already have your domain name registered with a company that does not seem to be the best fit for your hosting, no worries, you can have your domain name registered anywhere and it is super easy to redirect (point) to any hosting company.

Choosing a Hosting Plan

Now that we have chosen our hosting company, we can purchase our hosting plan. So which one? This will vary greatly depending on your needs and the type of website you plan on building. If you are going to build a regular informational website and expect moderate traffic to the site, then you can get away with a basic Linux-based cPanel hosting package, middle tier or higher. Keep in mind that most of all the new websites can expect low to moderate traffic in the beginning unless you have a strong marketing team already in place.

If you are planning on building an ecommerce website (selling products and getting paid on your website) then I would recommend the upper tier. If you plan on a very large ecommerce website then you will require a VPS (Virtual Private Server) package. A large ecommerce site is anything more than, say, 25 or so products. If you do need a VPS package, then I would suggest a lower- to middle-tier package, because unlike the regular hosting packages, you can upgrade at any time to increase resources. Because VPS is "virtual," it is a matter of the hosting company allocating more resources, and it does not require moving the website to a different server. Now if you only plan on ever having five to ten pages, then you can choose the lowest tier in Linux-based cPanel hosting.

Don't get caught up in the tech specs of each tier, as it can and will blow your mind. A hosting company is essentially renting you computer space on a server, much like subletting an apartment in a large building. This is what we call "shared hosting," because there may be a lot of other hosting accounts on any server. All of these hosting plans are like the one you will buy, and you all share the same resources from the server. The server is nothing more than a fancy name for a strong computer, so when you think of resources, think of your own computer. The resources refer to the speed of the processor, the amount of RAM and, of course, the memory or hard drive. The processor speed, RAM and available memory to store things greatly affect the speed of your computer doing tasks, and those same resources either keep you running smoothly or can slow down your website. This is why I seldom recommend lower-tier hosting plans. VPS has a lot more resources and is easily scaled or increased, so I always refer to lower tiers that you can add to later or scale up should you need to.

I do understand this can be confusing, but if you are in doubt, call your host and say that you are planning to build a Wordpress website and want a Linux-based cPanel hosting account. Tell the host how big you think your site will be in terms of pages and/or products you will be selling and they can help steer you in the right direction. Just be sure to stay away from hosting packages like "Wordpress Hosting" or options geared toward or "optimized for" Wordpress in general. Over the years, I have found that these types of Wordpress optimized hosting plans are very limiting and make it hard to perform more advanced functions on your Wordpress website or do anything in general that requires access to the source code. You will be better off with your Linux-based cPanel hosting plan that most closely fits your needs, not features with bells and whistles that they mark up and push with name recognition.

You Don't Need It

Now that you've chosen the hosting company, domain name and hosting plan for your business website, we need to discuss how to purchase it. It is a shame I even have to bring this up, but some hosting companies will try to push products on you that you flat-out do not need (like Wordpress Optimized Hosting). You do not need to "protect your privacy" with your domain name, you do not need Google listing anything. These products may sound great, but they are a huge waste of money! The only thing you need in your cart when you check out is your hosting and perhaps your domain name.

Don't be fooled by sale prices on hosting plans. The "sale" price is almost always based on buying several years' worth of service at once. Though they advertise and make it seem as though you will pay $6.99 a month, if you look closely, you'll see that you are required to buy 24 months or more upfront to get that price. With that said, if you are comfortable with it, I would suggest the two-year hosting plan with the annual domain name plan. Two years is usually enough to get the best discount. But if there is no extreme discount (say, 40 percent or more) for going long term, then I would opt for a month-to-month or quarterly plan.

Once you are in the cart and ready to check out, double-check that the hosting company did not throw anything else in the cart that you did not add yourself. Always pay attention to the number of years included in the price — many times the hosting company will auto-add the maximum.

Remember: If there is ever a need for additional services, you can always purchase them later. Buying things you really do not need and then trying to get a refund is a pain in the backside!

Setting Up cPanel

Once you check out, most hosting companies require you to "set up" your cPanel. cPanel is, as you may have guessed, the control panel for your hosting. cPanel allows you to do a ton of stuff besides your website, including host your own email . . . for free. Now proceed to set up your cPanel with the hosting company's interface or setup wizard. You will be asked for the domain name and to create a password for the cPanel.

Once completed, go to your cPanel and take a quick look around. Though cPanel is a licensed software, some hosts change the look and may restrict some of the tools inside, but you will have everything you need to create your Wordpress website and email. I encourage you to take a video tour through cPanel by visiting my tutorials on Yourtube "Learning Wordpress for Businesses." The cPanel video tutorial is found here: https://youtu.be/PvYxoDpnKec

Setting Up Email Inside cPanel

Now that you have cPanel setup, we can create a domain email for free. A domain email is simply an email address using your domain name. For example: My domain name is integritywebstudios.com and my personal email address is shane@integritywebstudios.com. This not only adds to your website's professional appearance, but it is also adds an extra level of trust, as anyone can make a free email account with Gmail or Yahoo, and a lot of spam is created using these free email accounts. There are limitations to cPanel email, but you can run three to five email addresses for years under regular circumstances. For example, I still use cPanel for my company email.

Scroll down to or find the "Email" section inside cPanel and click on the "Email Accounts" icon. Once inside you will be pleased to find a simple wizard to allow you to create an email address. You simply add the prefix or name of the email address you are creating. (For example, mine is "shane.") Below that you must choose the domain name for creating the email (If you only have one, then it will be selected) and create a password. In the quota section, simply select "unlimited" and hit the "Create Account" button. That's it!! Easy, right?

Now that the email has been created, you may create as many email addresses as you like. BUT keep in mind that while they allow unlimited email addresses, they do not have unlimited resources. See how they get you? So running a handful of email addresses is fine, but running 15 email addresses will take a byte (pun intended) out of your resources and will affect the speed of your website. In the cases where you need many email addresses, I highly recommend G-Suite from Google, or if you are a Microsoft person, then perhaps Microsoft Office 365. Both offer Cloud-based domain email services, a suite of productivity products like spreadsheets, text editors and so on, and range between $5 and $7 per email address.

Now that the emails have been created, scroll down to see the list of emails you have made below the wizard. Next to each email are a few action options such as "Change/Reset Password," "Setup Email Client," "Delete" and a "More" button. Click the "More" button to reveal a dropdown and you will see an "Access Webmail" option. Click that and it will take you to the cPanel webmail handler — basically, a page where you can choose one of three open source email clients. I prefer "RoundCube," but you can choose any of them. Once inside, you can send, receive and manage all email for this domain. Pretty nifty, huh? You can access your email by visiting your domain name with "/webmail" on the end. For example: YourDomainName.com/webmail. Your username will be the full email address and, of course, the password is the one you made when you created the email.

To use a third-party email client such as Mac Mail, Outlook, Gmail, or Yahoo, click on your email address in the top right from inside your email and select "Configure Mail Client" from the dropdown. An email client is simply a program that you use to send, receive and manage your email.

Alternatively, you may access this link in several places as well as in the email accounts section where we created the emails. This opens a page with all the information you need to add your email to any other email client. Each email client is different, so you will have to find instructions from each for that specific email client, except for those listed at the top of the page. Those links are auto-setup scripts that will set it up for you. Just make sure you open the "Configure Mail Client" page on the device to which you wish to add your domain email, then click the link and follow the wizard. All other email clients such as Google, Yahoo and so on will require a manual setup. The information needed can be found below setup scripts.

PLEASE NOTE: Be sure to use the information labeled "Non-SSL Settings (NOT Recommended)" when manually setting up an email client. Unless you purchase an SSL certificate, you do not have this security, nor do you need it.

SSL is only required if you are building an ecommerce website.

Installing Wordpress

At this point we have our domain name, hosting company, cPanel and email address all nailed down. If you do not have all of these at this point, please stop and go back to complete all of these steps. Once completed, come back to this chapter. The reason we are being sticklers for order here is that you need each one of these in place to get your website up and running, and failing to have one of these completed will have you at a standstill.

Easy Installation

One of the reasons I am so adamant about cPanel is that *most* hosting companies' cPanels come with an auto-install script. In layman's terms, this means there is a wizard that will walk you through your Wordpress website installation and setup. This is a great tool, and you should use it if you have it in your cPanel. Right now, I know that GoDaddy,

Inmotion Hosting and Bluehost all have an auto-install script for Wordpress inside cPanel. If you are not with any of these hosting companies, be sure to look for it inside your cPanel or call your hosting company. If you do not have it, don't worry, we will go through the manual installation steps together and you may skip this section to go to the "Manual Installation" section.

Inside your cPanel, scroll down to find the "Software" or "Applications" section. Inside Inmotion Hosting it will be "Software" and the installer is called "Softaculous." If you are inside GoDaddy, then it will be in "Applications" and the installer is called "Installatron." Inside Bluehost it is under the "Website" section and the installer is called "One-Click Installs." In either setting, get to your installer and select Wordpress from the available frameworks. The installer will then behave as a wizard tool, asking you to answer several questions similar to the following Inmotion Hosting and GoDaddy questions:

> **Domain:** Enter your domain name
> **Choose Protocol:** Simply select "http://"

Directory: Always leave empty (you may have to delete auto-created location like "blog")
GoDaddy Only:
    Version: Use defaults or "recommended"
    Language: Select language if not English
    Auto Updates: Use default settings
Blog Name: Your Company Name
Blog Tagline: A Company Tagline (this is a required field so use the blog name if you have nothing now. Don't worry, you can change it later if you want.)
Multisite: Nope, you don't want this
Admin Username: Create a user name
Admin Password: Create password (make it strong!!!!!)
Admin Email: This will be used to send your messages, and if you ever need to reset password (it is not shown to public)
Limit Login Attempts: Yes, please

Click "Install" and let the script do the rest. Be sure to write your username and password in the back of the book for easy reference and safekeeping. Once the script finishes, you will be presented with the final two links to your new website: the frontend link and the backend link. The "frontend" is the public-facing side of your website — basically, what the rest of the world will see when they land on your website. The "backend" is essentially inside the CMS where only those who have a username and password can access. As an example, consider restaurateurs' jargon:

"front of house" versus "back of house." "Front of house" simply refers to where the customers sit, order and/or dine. "Back of house" refers to the kitchen and other areas off-limits to customers. Frontend/backend is the same concept, and exclusive to websites for our purposes.

Manual Installation

If you are reading this, then it is likely you do not have the quick-install scripts in your cPanel. No worries. You will have the unique opportunity to get a head start in understanding how your Wordpress website works. Again, this is much easier than expected but does require several steps. Let's get started!

Get the Files

First, we need to download the Wordpress file stack. We do this by visiting wordpress.org and clicking the blue "Download Wordpress" button. You will download a zip file that is named wordpress-vx.x.x.zip (do not unzip it yet).

Since versions change often, I left it with a variable in the name, but you get the point. You will always get the latest stable version via the wordpress.org download page.

Upload the Files

Save those files to your desktop or a location you can get to easily. Now go back to your cPanel and click into "File Manager." Inside "File Manager," navigate your way to the "public_html" folder. Sometimes the hosting company will put you there automatically and sometimes you are in the root of the site. ("Root" simply means the base or lowest file possible — in other words, the beginning.) If you are in the root you will see a folder "public_html" and have to click into it. If you find yourself in a folder with only another folder labeled "cgi-bin," then you are likely already inside the public _html folder. You can check by viewing the site tree to your left.

At the top of the page, look for an "Upload" button and upload the zip file just as you downloaded it (still zipped).

Once you have uploaded the file, you may be prompted to "Go Back" or you can simply close the upload page and go back to the public_html folder. If you do not see the Wordpress zip file, click the "Reload" icon at the top of the page. If you still do not see the file, be sure you are in the right folder "public_html" and if need be, reupload again.

Click on the icon of the zip file and then right click and select "Extract." This will prompt a dialogue box that will ask where you want to extract the files to. Simply select "Extract Files," keeping the same location. Again, you may need to reload the page using the reload icon at the top to see the extracted file folder name "Wordpress." Click into the Wordpress folder and at the top of the page, click the "Select All" button. Alternatively, you can hold "Command" and click to select them individually on a Mac, and in Windows it is "Ctrl" and click. Once every file is highlighted, click the "Move" button at the top of the page. A dialogue box will open and you will then edit the file path to send the files where you want to move them. In our case, we are simply moving the files into the public_html folder. We should be inside the Wordpress folder, so all we need to do is delete the "/wordpress" from the end of the file path. It should now read "/public_html." Click "Move Files." You will see the files disappear; if you missed one, repeat until all files are gone. Now click the "Up One Level" button at the top and you should be back in the public_html folder along with all the files. We can now delete the zip package file and the empty Wordpress folder from where we just moved the files.

Creating the Database

Now that the files are present inside the public_html folder, we need to go back to cPanel and scroll to find the "Database" section. Inside the Database section we will find the "MySQL Database Wizard." Select that. Once inside the wizard we will be prompted to answer a few simple questions. We will need to create a database name. Once we create the name, click the "Next Step" button to create a Database User. Same thing here: We will give it a name, but this only allows for a maximum of seven characters.

Next, create a strong password, a VERY strong password. There will be a password generator, and it can create a password strong enough to use. In any case, as long as your password passes the strength indicator, you are fine. Now click the "Next Step" button below. Paste your password somewhere you can easily get to it. You will need it in a moment. The third and final step of the database wizard is to set "Privileges" for the user. In our case, we want to select the top box to "Select All." Alternatively, you may select them all one by one. Click the "Next Step" button and you are done.

Setting Up Config File

Now that we have our database name, database username and password, we can go back to the public_html folder inside file manager. Scroll down to find the file "wp-config-sample.php." The first thing we need to do is rename this file to "wp-config.php" by simply clicking on the name twice and then deleting the "-sample" in the name, then hitting "Enter." Once the file is renamed, click on the icon and then right click to select "Edit" or the "Code Edit" link.

PLEASE NOTE: If you have both "Edit" and "Code Edit" options, be sure to select "Code Edit."

This will open the file and allow you to edit the code inside. You may be prompted by a dialogue box asking if you would like to change encoding or asking to disable encoding check. Just click the "Edit" button or the "Ignore Encoding Check" to view the file.

Once inside the wp-config.php file, scroll to the database settings and we will simply copy and paste our info where it is called for. It will look like this:

```
// ** MySQL settings - You can get this info from your
web host ** //
/** The name of the database for WordPress */
define('DB_NAME', 'database_name_here');

/** MySQL database username */
define('DB_USER', 'username_here');

/** MySQL database password */
define('DB_PASSWORD', 'password_here');

/** MySQL hostname */
define('DB_HOST', 'localhost');
```

- 43 -

```
/** Database Charset to use in creating database
tables. */
define('DB_CHARSET', 'utf8');

/** The Database Collate type. Don't change this if in
doubt. */
define('DB_COLLATE', '');
```

We ONLY need to edit the top three for the database name,

username and password, all of which we just created.

PLEASE NOTE: Be sure to paste the information INSIDE

the quotation marks.

Once completed, click the blue "Save Changes" button at the

top right of the editor.

Now that you have saved the database information, scroll

down to the "Authentication Unique Keys and Salts" section,

as shown below. Notice that in the green text (the green text

in code editors signifies that it is comment information only

and not part of the code) there is a link:

https://api.wordpress.org/secret-key/1.1/salt/. Copy the link

and paste it into your browser in a new tab or page. You will get a bunch of crazy-looking characters that are laid out

behind the word "define." These are encryption keys, and

every time you hit "Refresh," you will see that it generates a

new, unique set of them. Simply copy EVERYTHING and go

back to your open wp-config.php file and select the generic

placeholder keys (select the word "Define" and all default

info text and paste over that with the new salt keys you just

copied. No need to copy only the key and paste in only in the

"put your unique phrase here." We can select the whole

chunk and paste over it for simplicity. If you would like to

watch a video walk-through of exactly what we are copying

and pasting, you can view my video tutorial on Youtube. At

the 6:40 time marker I show you how to select and paste the

salt keys. https://youtu.be/Lim8SYh5mrE

Once pasted, hit the "Save Changes" button at the top right

of the editor and test the site by typing your domain name

into your browser. You should see a Wordpress setup page.

If you see only a white screen with the text "error

establishing a database connection," then double-check your

database information inside the wp-config.php file. If

everything looks correct and you still have the error, try

resetting your database user password inside the "MySQL

Databases" section in cPanel. If you see the Wordpress

setup page, then we are done inside cPanel.

```
/**#@+
 * Authentication Unique Keys and Salts.
 *
 * Change these to different unique phrases!
 * You can generate these using the {@link
https://api.wordpress.org/secret-key/1.1/salt/
WordPress.org secret-key service}
 * You can change these at any point to invalidate all
existing cookies. This will force all users to have to
log in again.
 *
 * @since 2.6.0
 */
define('AUTH_KEY',        'put your unique phrase
here');
define('SECURE_AUTH_KEY', 'put your unique
phrase here');
define('LOGGED_IN_KEY',   'put your unique
phrase here');
define('NONCE_KEY',       'put your unique
phrase here');
define('AUTH_SALT',       'put your unique phrase
here');
define('SECURE_AUTH_SALT', 'put your unique
phrase here');
define('LOGGED_IN_SALT',  'put your unique
phrase here');
define('NONCE_SALT',      'put your unique
phrase here');
```

Completing the Wordpress Installation

Now that we have landed on the setup page, it will first ask you to choose your language from a dropdown. From the first question, you probably have already guessed that this is yet another helpful wizard tool. Simply complete the setup and when finished you will see a success message and a button to "Log In." You have officially finished setting up your Wordpress website. If you visit the frontend of the website, now you will see the default theme used by Wordpress.

You Did It!

Its official! Give yourself a high five and do a dance, you have just finished setting up your website framework. You officially have a website live on the Internet. Though we do technically have a website, right now it is too generic and incomplete to be used for your business. Let's continue and get to designing.

Logging In to Your New Wordpress Website

To get to our backend, simply go to your browser and type in your URL (domain name). For example, "YourDomainName.com" and add a "/wp-admin" to the end of your URL with no spaces. It should look like this: "YourDomainName.com/wp-admin"

Your website will automatically forward you to the login page, which is actually "YourDomainName.com/wp-login.php." No need to save this info, but I mention it just so you know why you see a different URL when you are actually on the login page. At this point you will enter your username and password that you created when you set up Wordpress. Once inside the Wordpress CMS you will land on the dashboard page. Notice all the navigation links

(**PLEASE NOTE:** I will use the the term "nav" or "nav item" intermittently with the term "navigation links") on the left-hand side of the page. This is where the magic happens. Every page of your website, every article and every image will be added right here in the CMS.

The Wordpress CMS

You will always land on the dashboard page once you log in to your CMS. For the most part, that is the extent of its use, although later, when you have plugins and other functions working, it will also give you some quick info relative to the various plugins, such as sales reports or new lead generations and so on. I will give you an overview of the CMS, but keep in mind that I will be skipping around to cover functions and tools.

PLEASE NOTE: This overview is by no means exhaustive, but understanding a handful of the many tools is more than enough to design, develop, edit and update your Wordpress website.

Getting Around

The first thing I like to point out to clients is the black "Admin" bar that is at the very top of the page. It is a minimal 32 pixels high strip of black that runs across the top of the page. If you look to the far left inside the "Admin" bar you will see a home icon and the name of your website. If you click on that it will send you to the homepage on the frontend of your website. Click that now. Notice that you are on the homepage and you still see the black "Admin" bar. Only logged-in users will see the "Admin" bar. Now the icon has changed to a speedometer on the front end but the name is the same. If you click on it now it will take you to the backend dashboard page.

Later, when we add pages to our website, there will be an additional link inside the "Admin" bar that will take you from frontend to backend and vice versa, except it is for the specific post or page that you are on at that time.

If you are logged in to your website and on the frontend, you can navigate to a webpage using regular on-page navigation, and in the "Admin" bar you will see a link to "Edit Page." Clicking on that will bring you to the backend editor for that page and not the dashboard. Same thing if you are in the backend editing a page, you will see a link to "View Page" that when clicked takes you to that page on the frontend. Trust me, this will save you time later when you are developing your website.

Redundancies

You will find that it is very common to have redundancies or many different ways of doing the same thing in Wordpress. This is normal and in fact, a great web practice for any high-quality website. For example: hovering or clicking on a nav item will both show a submenu (secondary level of navigation links nested under the primary nav item). *If* there is one for that section. You may choose to hover and wait for the flyout to reveal the navigation items you may go to or simply click the primary item and the submenu will be pulled down and seated below the nav item. In short, just know that there are many ways to perform the same task, so if you find one I don't mention or like one that I did not talk about, no worries, use it well.

Users

Navigate to the backend of the site and from the dashboard look to the navigation on the left of the page and find "Users." Clicking "Users" or "All Users" is the same function (remember redundancies) and will place you in the Users section. From here you can manage the users of your website. Now you are the only user and will be the only user you see, but just know that every user (including customers if you have an ecommerce website) will be found and controlled here. For our needs, this is just to show you where you can go to create a new user, reset passwords or complete your profile. If you click on your username (or hover and click "Edit") you will land inside that user profile. Usernames are not allowed to be changed, but everything else can be edited. The only required fields to create a new user are the username, email address, password and the "Role" or privileges, from the least privileges to the greatest. Roles are defined as follows:

Subscriber: somebody who can manage only his or her profile.

Contributor: somebody who can write and manage his or her own posts but cannot publish them.

Author: somebody who can publish and manage his or her own posts.

Editor: somebody who can publish and manage posts including the posts of other users.

Administrator: somebody who has access to all the administration features within a site.

There is one more default role, but you will not see this unless you are running a multisite setup.

Super Admin: somebody with access to the site network administration features and all other features.

It is worth noting that there is a box that, when selected, will email a newly created user his or her username and password automatically.

All users who forget their passwords can initiate an automated reset password function that will email a reset link to the email address on file for that user. This link is found right below the login box on the wp-admin page and as of today is worded, "Lost your password?"

Settings

General Settings

Now let's jump to "Settings," which is usually a few items below "Users." When we click "Settings" or the flyout submenu item "General," it takes us to the same place. Here is where you can rename your website, change your tagline, allow or disallow users to register, and where you will set the date and time for your region.

Writing Settings

Though I never use these settings (I personally change default category in the category section, not in settings), I will briefly explain what they do. Here we can set the following:

Default Post Category: the category that will be given to a post unless you assign another category when creating it.

Default Post Format: a way of defining the default style of a post unless assigned when creating.

Post Via Email Setup: once setup, this allows you to post directly to your website by emailing the information.

Updating Services: when a new post is added, an updating service will automatically notify subscribers of new information on the website.

Reading Settings

Again, I seldom make changes inside this setting because there is another location to set the "front page." Here we can define the page we want to be the "front page" (this is the way Wordpress describes the homepage of our website). By default, Wordpress is set to dynamically add your "Posts" or articles to a page that you can choose. This setting is the "Your latest post." This is **not** the setting that we see operating on most websites. This is the setting to choose if you are simply creating a blog. If you want to create the website for your business, then we will likely require the normal website formatting of choosing a "static page" for the front page (homepage). There is no need to mess with these settings yet as we do not have any pages created.

Discussion Settings

Here we can set up how our discussions, comments and notifications for both are handled. Under the "Default Article Settings" I recommend unchecking "Allow Link Notifications . . . ." and "Allow People to Post . . . ." This is where you can allow comments on your articles, which again is great if you are blogging. However, we do not need that function and it is notorious for all kinds of spam comments and advertisements. Since comments and discussions are not our main goal, we are eliminating it altogether. Needless to say, should you add a blog or news section to your business website and want to allow people to comment, then here is where you can change it back any time.

Media Settings

This is where we can control the sizes of our thumbnails and how to organize the media once uploaded. Leave this at the default settings. When you upload any image to your website through the CMS, the website automatically creates three different sizes of that image to make it easier to create content. So for any image uploaded you will have four different sizes to choose from in adding it to your pages: Thumbnail, Medium, Large, and full size.

Permalinks Settings

Here is where we can edit the look of our links. This is how we change weird URLs into easy-to- remember and more meaningful URLs. By default Wordpress creates URLs to your various pages with ID numbers. This is not the most meaningful or easiest way to remember the URL, and Wordpress was wise enough to incorporate an interface that allows you to take control of it. This easy-to-read URL also benefits SEO (search engine optimization), or getting found by search engines organically. In short, you will see several settings to choose from. I highly recommend selecting the "Post Name" option if it is not selected by default. If we have a page created on our website called "How to Remember Your URL" it will turn the URL from something like this:

YourDomainName.com/p_id_712398

Into something like this:

YourDomainName.com/how-to-remember-your-url

Pages

Inside your CMS, navigate to "Pages." Whether you click on the main nav item "Pages" or the sub nav menu item "All Pages," you will be able to list all of your pages on the website. Since we only just installed our website, we are likely to see only a "Sample Page" created by the Wordpress framework when we installed the website. Notice at the top there is an "Add New" button and below that you will see two links to show selected page groups, "Published" and "Trash."

We don't need a lot of explanation here, but pages you put in the trash are immediately removed from the frontend so users cannot access them, but are not deleted until you actually "empty trash" from inside the trash section on the backend.

PLEASE NOTE: Due to the nature of Wordpress and its dependence upon themes to add style and layout, it is literally impossible to cover every aspect of what a page's content area *may* offer. We will discuss a few of the core functions of a Wordpress page, but this is by no means exhaustive.

Add a New Page

To add a new page we can select "Add New" from inside the "Pages" view or alternatively, once logged in to your website, the admin bar at the top of the page (front or backend) will have a "+ New" section that when hovered over will reveal a list of items that you can create for, one of which is a "page."

In either case, let's click on one and you will see a new blank page will open up.

Title

The page is again pretty self-explanatory, but it is worth noting a few key features. We clearly have a title area at the top of the page. The title of the page is one of the most important elements on the page as it will not only define the "<h1>" heading (the most important heading on a page that tells users and search engines the main topic of the page). It will also create a navigation item that we can later use to create our website navigation menu.

Content Area (Text Editor)

Below the title field we find the content area. This is where the rubber meets the road, so to speak, with our website. We will design and build our pages and write content in this section on every page. The first thing I would like to point out is to the right on the top of the content editor you will find two tabs, "Visual" and "Text." You will live in the "Visual" version of the editor. This is the editor that works as any other text editor you may have used (like Word). We type in plain English and if we want to mark up any of our text such as make it bold, italic or add a link to it, we simply highlight the text we want to mark up and click the appropriate icon above that will add that markup to the text. There should be two rows of icons at the top of the editor. If you only see one then hover over the icons to find the "Toggle Toolbar" and it will reveal the remaining icons/functions. There is also an "Add Media" button at the top left above the content area. In our case I will spend a few minutes discussing this in greater detail in the next chapter. Essentially, there are two main features we will use a lot and that require a bit of extra knowledge in order to deliver a high-quality SEO-sound website.

Adding a Link on a Page or Post

In the case of adding a link, we would highlight the text that we want to make a link and click the "Chain Link" icon in the toolbar above the content area. Once clicked, a popup will appear to help us build the link. A basic link has a few elements that you should understand. Whether a link is a button or textual (the only difference between a textual link and a button is styling), it will have the same key elements to make it a high-quality link that users and search engines will appreciate.

URL: the destination link

Link Text: the words that are shown to the user and are clicked on to send to the destination, for example: "Click Here."

Target: two basic link targets used in Wordpress are "_blank" and "_self."

"_blank" will open the link in a new tab or page while leaving your web page up. We use this exclusively when we have to send users to a web page that is **NOT** in our website. We never want to send a user anywhere except within our website, but if we must link out we want to make sure that the page does not replace your page but opens in a new page.

"_self" will replace the page the user is on with the new page. All other links within your website will get the attribute "_self."

The good news is you will not have to deal with any of the coding works of building a link. Wordpress will launch a popup that allows you to paste the link into the field, and to complete the link you simply click the blue "Enter" icon to the right of the field. This is for any link within your website. However, if you need to link out, then you may click the "Gear" icon to the right of the "Enter" icon and it will open the legacy — tech speak for older version — Wordpress dialogue. This dialogue will ask for or have an option for the "Link Text," "URL," and an "Open Link in a New Tab" check box to select if you are linking away from your website. If you are linking within your website there is a list of all your existing website pages below this, and by clicking on the page or post you want to link out to, it will automatically fill in the URL and "Link Text" for you.

Adding an Image on a Page or Post

PLEASE NOTE: We will first need to process our images before uploading simply as a good practice, but preprocessing is not required, only recommended. We will discuss preprocessing images in the next chapter.

The next thing I would like to walk through is the "Add Media" button above the content editor. We use this to . . . .

You guessed it, we use this to add images. For the most part it is pretty straightforward. We place our cursor where we would like the image to go and then click the "Add Media" button. This then opens a page that allows you to do a few different things. We can upload a new image (or media file such as MP3), we can browse our media library for an image that has already been uploaded, or we can create an image gallery. Whether we upload an image or select it from our library of already uploaded images, we have a few things we need to learn before adding it to our page. Once you have selected or uploaded the image you want, it will have a blue outline on the thumbnail of the image along with a blue box that has a check in it. This clearly indicates that you have selected that image. You can click on another image and it will deselect the image you originally chose and select the new one. If you would like to insert more than one image, simply hold "Command" as you click on a Mac and "Ctrl" as you click on a Windows PC. Once you have an image selected, on the top right side of the page you will see some information about the image. Below this information you will

- 64 -

find some info fields. Here is a brief description of what they do:

URL: This is the direct path to the actual file inside your website. If you copy the URL and paste in a browser you will see only the image.

Title: The text you want to see when you hover your mouse over an image or button.

Caption: This is an explanation or description of the image that will be displayed below the image. No, still doesn't make sense — is there a way to distinguish between the 2 images in both sentences, this + one below?

Alt Text: A brief explanation of the image that is only shown when the user cannot see the image for any reason. Created for ADA compliance (special systems for the blind would read this text to them), it also benefits the onsite SEO.

Description: This is an explanation of the image if it were opened via the "attachment page," which we will discuss later.

Below this information you will find one more group of settings:

Alignment: This allows you to select how the image will be laid out. Think of a newspaper or magazine article that has images in it.
>**Left:** When this is selected we will see the image to the left with the text wrapping neatly around the image on the right side.

Right: When this is selected we see the image far right with the text wrapping to the left side.

Center: When this is selected the image will float center and the text will be neatly wrapped to the right and left.

None: Simply means no alignment will be used.

Link to: This allows us to use the image as a link. **Custom URL:** Copy and paste any URL in the field below to link to it when the image is clicked.

Attachment Page: The image will open on a page within your website with nothing on the page except the image and the description, if you created one.

Media File: The image will open up on a new tab/page in your browser independent of your website. It is the same as copying and pasting the media URL into the browser.

None: The image is not linked to anything

Size: When adding media to a Wordpress website, the website will automatically make three different size variations of that image. These size variations may differ widely between different themes. As an example, I will show you the pixel sizes on my personal website (which were likely created by the theme, as I almost never edit the media upload settings).

Full Size: The actual size uploaded

Large: 1024 x 795

Medium: 300 x 233

Thumbnail: 150 x 150

My recommendations when you upload an image are to first "crop" (trim) the image to the correct size for which you want to use it. Then to "Optimize the Image for Web," and finally, to save the image with a meaningful name (for example: a picture of the Eiffel Tower may be saved as Eiffel Tower Paris France.jpg). This is part of the preprocessing that we will discuss in a few chapters.

Once you upload the image, you will need to add the "Alt Text" description. Many times the "title" that is auto-populated by Wordpress based on the file name can simply be copied and pasted as the "Alt Text" as long as there are no hyphens and it is appropriately capitalized. Then select the alignment you would like, select "None" for link (unless you want to link the image) and then choose the size (which should be full size because we cropped it before uploading it). Then hit the blue "Insert Into Page" button. The page will close, placing you back inside the editor, and the new image will be visible. Hit the blue "Publish" or "Update" button ("Update" is visible if you have already published the page). Once the page refreshes, there will be a "View Page" link at the top inside the admin bar and on the page. Click that to view what you just uploaded to make sure the layout is what you intended.

PLEASE NOTE: I always recommend to even the most advanced Wordpress users to save ("Update" or "Save Draft)" often and always check the page immediately after saving to ensure that it looks and behaves as expected. I have learned this lesson hard way!

Cool Stuff You Should Know

The next few things I will point out are simply cool things you may find useful in your Wordpress website for your business. The first is going to be found right above the "Publish" or

"Update" button. There will be a box labeled "Publish" that has a few of these cool options in it. Let's take a look.

Publish Tools

Status: This shows the status of the webpage you are on and has three options; it is pretty self-explanatory. It is worth mentioning that a page must be "published" for it to be seen on the frontend of the website.

Visibility: This setting determines how the page is seen and also has three options.

> **Public:** Any user on the front end of the website can see the page.
>
> **Private:** The web page is only viewable if you are logged in to the website. Remember, your website allows many different user roles besides administrator.
>
> **Password Protected:** The page is only viewable after you enter a password, which you create after you select this option in the backend. If users do not have the password, they will not see the page.

Publish: This option allows you to publish the page immediately or set an exact time and date to publish it. Great for new content, product or promotional pages.

Pretty neat stuff and very useful at times. One other tool I will bring up is the "Revisions" on a page.

Revisions

Revisions are saved copies of every edit that was ever saved on the webpage you are on. Let me say that again . . . . EVERY edit that was ever saved on the page.

Wordpress has this beautiful feature to save you from yourself. Sometimes when we edit a page and save it, it does not come out the way we want or expected it to. Remember I said to get in the habit of checking your work and saving often? This is the solution for when the work you expected is not what you see. "Revisions" is usually found on the bottom of the page. If you do not see a section called "Revisions," scroll back to the very top of the page and at the very top right, protruding down from the admin bar, you will see a tab called "Screen Options." Click that tab and a list of items with checkboxes next to them will appear. Look for "Revisions" and click the box next to it. All items checked off are visible on your backend page view. Now simply scroll back down to find the "Revisions" section. You will see a list of revisions with the editor's name (this will be you since no one else has edited it yet), as well as the date/time, and how long ago the edit was saved.

So if you ever goof up and need to go back, this is your magic reset button. Simply select the last stable version of content you would like to go to and the page will open a difference comparison table to show you **exactly** what the difference is in the pages with highlighted text. You can simply choose "Restore This Version" and then hit "Update" and you are good to go.

Auto-Save

There is a built-in auto-save function for pages and posts, though I would suggest you not depend on it. It is a great tool and pretty stable in that it works well. However, best practices of saving often are by far the best insurance to preserve your work. Remember that your work is being saved to the Cloud (otherwise known as the Internet), so we will always be required to be online in order for **any** changes to be saved.

Posts

A post is just like a page on a website except it is specifically built for articles and blogs. A post will not only have the content areas but also, a lot of "meta" information ("meta" simply means "along with" but you can consider it as "extra info" and is used by search engines including the website's own search function) so that the articles can be easily archived and searched. The beauty of Wordpress is that any post you create will automatically be archived by the website. Another amazing feature is that we can create categories and separate the articles with them.

As an example, a tourist website may create categories for "Hotels," "Restaurants" and "Entertainment." As the website creates weekly articles, it can simply create a single post and select which category/categories the article goes under. They can now separate the articles by the categories if they like. So we could create a page for each category, and when a user goes to that page, he or she will see a list of all the articles written for that category only. This is where the meta information comes in, as it will have the author, posted date and category info. A user simply clicks on the title and the article opens up. This is the core functionality of Wordpress and why it was created.

Posts are built out exactly like pages on your website, except we have a few key extras that we will dive into — which is essentially the meta information. So just like the page, we will have a title, content area and publish options. There will also be a place to add "Tags," or keywords that a user can search that may be relevant to the article's topic. We can choose categories from a list that we have already created or simply create a new category on the spot by clicking the "Add New Category" link. Once we click the link, we see a field to add a new category name. Simply click the button below "Add New Category" and you will see it show up in the list automatically selected.

Another difference will be the "Featured Image." This is usually found below the "Publish" or "Update" button on the right side. The featured image will automatically be the header (sometimes called banner image) and is the main image — usually the largest of all images and usually found at the top of the page. The website also creates a thumbnail image when the website archive is shown. Be sure to stick with your dimensions when using the featured image. As a designer, I cringe when I see thumbnails that are slightly irregular because the featured image size changed. Keep in mind that different themes will have different layouts and styles to display the posts lists within the "blog page," so be sure to pay attention to this when you choose your theme.

Navigation Menu

The navigation menu, which I refer to as "menu" or "nav menu" but listed in Wordpress as "Menus"), is the main menu that shows buttons or textual links to navigate around the website. Typically found at the top of the page for best web practices, the nav menu is easy to create and edit. The first thing you should understand about the nav menu is that for every page you create on your website, a nav menu item is created for it automatically. To view the list of nav items and build out your website's navigation, we will go to "Appearances > Menus." Once you are here we can begin learning how to create our nav menu for the website.

Create Your Website's Navigation Menu

Once on the "Menus" page you will see a list of the pages you have already created on your website in a section called "Pages," on the far left. Notice that there are tabs within that section for "Most Recent," "View All," and "Search." Clicking on the check box to the left of each page name in that section to select the item/s and then clicking "Add to Menu" will automatically add those items to the menu, which is the main section of the page found to the right of the "Pages."

Before we can add nav items to our menu, we first need to create a menu or select the menu we want to build. It is common to have several different menus for different areas of the website. For example, the footer menu may be different from the main menu, while some websites have a "top bar" that looks similar to our admin bar but has nav menu links and other info. If you have more than one menu created already, you will see a dropdown to select the menu found right above the menu and pages area.

If you try to add pages to your menu by selecting the box and clicking "Add to Menu" and it won't allow it, you will need to create a menu by simply clicking the textual link "Create a New Menu." Give it a name and click the blue "Create Menu" button. Once that has been created, you may add to the menu. After you have added the pages to the main menu, they will appear in the main section. You must now select a checkbox below the menu you are on in the "Menu Settings" to place it as the main menu, or other menu location if your theme offers. Next, hit "Save Menu." Now if you go to the front end of your website, you will see the menu you just created.

Organizing Your Navigation Menu

After your first inspection of the nav menu on the front end you may wonder how to rearrange these. The answer is simple and easy to do. Let's go back to the "Menus" section on the backend and select the menu we are rearranging if you have more than one. To rearrange we simply drag and drop the menu items listed in the main menu section. We can easily rearrange them in any order we like and even create subnav items, which are simply nested navigation items that are only revealed when the primary nav item is hovered on or clicked. To make a subnav item, we simply drag and drop it slightly to the right until it sticks in place. Most themes allow you to create subnav items up to three layers deep. Once you have rearranged the nav items, be sure to hit "Save Menu" before leaving the page.

Processing Images

As mentioned in the previous chapter, I highly recommend preprocessing your images before uploading them to your website. When we upload photos, we want them to be as light as possible — meaning the smallest possible file size we can get away with. If a file size is too small, we see poor-quality photos. If it is too big, you slow down your site unnecessarily. Wordpress image sizes vary by theme, but let's say we upload a 5,000 x 5,000-pixel image to the site. It will likely be around 6 megabytes in size and way too large to be shown on the website page. So what happens is that the browser will scale it down automatically to fit in the page. The problem with that is that it is still using the very large image, and though it may only be showing at 1200px wide, the browser must still upload the entire 5,000 x 5,0000 pixel image in order to show the smaller image.

For example, if I know I need a medium-sized image to fit into my layout, I do not need to upload an image any larger than that. This is when it is advised to crop the image before we upload it. Crop your images using a photo editor such as Photoshop (my favorite) or a free online photo editor like Pixlr.com.

PLEASE NOTE: I will discuss how to use Pixlr.com to crop and optimize since it is the free version of the two. If you have another photo editor, feel free to use it. Most editors are similar and will allow you to optimize an image for web.

We can find out our sizes for various images on our website by navigating to the "Settings" > "Media" section in the backend of our website. Make a note of these three dimensions, as you will use them often. Alternatively, you may use the "Inspect" tool that comes with the dev tools inside most browsers. Firefox has a better version called "Firebug," while Chrome and Safari have versions that do the same thing. Essentially, if you right-click on any element on a web page, a popup appears and there will be an option to "Inspect." This opens an editor that shows the code used for the element you are inspecting. If you do this with an image on the page, it will also show you the exact dimensions of the image. Now go to your photo editor of choice and "Open Image from Your Computer" (In Pixlr.com use the Editor, not the Express) and upload the image to the image editor.

Next we will simply crop the image to size by using the crop tool. When cropping be sure to constrain the proportions. Do not crop an image without constraining the proportions. This insures that the image maintains the original height-to-width ratio so the image is not stretched or squeezed. **Never squeeze or stretch an image,** no matter how slightly. It is very unprofessional and an indication of a low-quality website. If the image is not big enough no matter how much you like it, you must move on to another that works within the dimensions you have. We now need to save the image. In Pixlr when you save the image the editor will automatically open an "Optimize for Web" compression tool. Use the slider to bring down the quality. I always recommend between 30 percent and 40 percent, but it will vary by the image.

Basically, bring the quality down until you begin to see the degradation of the image, then bump it back up a notch. Now hit "Save."

Finally, when we save our images, use a naming system that is consistent and descriptive of the image. Using the same example from the previous chapter: Save the image with a meaningful name (for example: a picture of the Eiffel Tower may be saved as "Eiffel Tower Paris France.jpg"). This is good for SEO and it makes your job of adding the "Alt Text" a little quicker, as you can simply copy the image title that is already added by the site, which gets it from the file name.

Forms

Website forms are a must for any reputable website so users can easily get in touch with you. There are dozens of great form builders to help you design your website's contact form easily. My favorite plugin is called Contact Form 7, but it requires a bit of html experience to make the forms look professional, so I seldom recommend it to the Wordpress beginner. You will want a good drag-and-drop builder. These builders make it a snap to add new form fields, check boxes, dropdown forms and validated form fields (like checking that an email address is correct).

For a great drag-and-drop builder you may like Ninja Forms, Gravity Forms or WP Forms. Some of these have free versions, some are paid, but all are great for first-time form builders. Like many of my other recommendations, this is not exhaustive and there are new ones being developed every day, so if you find another form builder that works for you, go for it.

Themes

As discussed previously, themes add the style and functionality to your Wordpress website. Some people describe themes as templates, but I really do not like using that term. A template is a tool used to reproduce something with the same features, while a theme defines a set of tools and styles that **may** be applied. With such a dynamic library of features, an infinite choice of colors, and a customizable page layout, themes can hardly be described as templates.

So we understand that a theme basically defines your website's look and function, but in addition, it also does something so much more. Well — some themes do so much more. I will explain. I advocate for the use of "premium themes" as opposed to the free themes that are available directly from the Wordpress repository. First, let's learn about each.

Free Themes

When you setup your Wordpress framework, your new website will offer a very easy way to search for, preview and install thousands of themes for free, directly from the CMS of your website. Yup, you heard me: **FREE**. The problem I have found is that the free themes are all either poorly done or a "freemium." A freemium is a business model most commonly recognized in apps. Basically, it is free to use, but if you want the super-amazing stuff that it can do, it will require an upgrade, which, guess what . . . is not free.

Bummer, right?

It is my experience that buying a premium theme and having it in hand from the beginning is the best way to go. I also find that most freemium themes are not as good as a premium theme that is sold outright. Please keep in mind that this is certainly not without exceptions to the rule. I am simply speaking from my experience. Which has led me to avoid the free zone altogether. I go straight for the premium themes.

Premium Themes

A premium theme is essentially a paid theme from a third-party developer. Premium themes often have a lot more features and may be very specific to a service or industry. For example, there are hundreds of themes built around real estate alone. Some themes are built for Realtors and brokers, while others are built for property managers. Some themes are built to pull the MLS data directly from the MLS provider of choice, while some allow you to manually add the data for a custom but similar listing look. They will have tools specific to the industry, such as contact forms, property listings (manual or imported) and other industry-related plugins and tools. The point is, there is a whole genre of Wordpress themes just for this one industry. And there are hundreds of industry-specific genres out there for Wordpress themes.

In addition to industry-specific layouts, tools and functions, most premium themes come with demo content. Demo content is really the unspoken hero for the novice Wordpress builder. Though Wordpress is extremely user friendly and easy to learn, believe it or not, web design is very technical to set up and lay out **properly**. Add to this the fact that layout and design guidelines can change depending on your goals for the website. So there can be a bit of a gap between the person Wordpress was intended for and his or her ability to use it effectively.

The average person using Wordpress will not have any formal design or development education, much less a fundamental understanding of web best practices. In fact, most people can barely tell you what they like or want when it comes to design in general, but can only tell you when they see something they like. This is OK, and essentially the norm when it comes to design, especially when people have a great sense of design and style. This is the primary reason more people cannot build their own Wordpress websites. Setting up a layout for a specific purpose does not come easily when you are starting from scratch. These gap factors, as I call them, are all overcome by the use of demo content.

Demo Content

Most of today's premium themes come with demo content. Demo content is nothing more than a predefined bunch of website pages, copy (website text), features and images that are easy to import into a Wordpress website. Though the capability has been been part of Wordpress for years, it has come a long way in the last five years and is much more stable.

When you find a premium theme, odds are that it will have a live demo website so you can "test drive" the theme and get a feel for what features are built in and the different layout options. Most themes will have many different layouts and designs for you to choose from. Once purchased, these themes will usually allow you to import the exact demo that is on the their demo site.

This is the big deal that I was talking about and the thing that really gives an advantage to the novice Wordpress user. This feature can save you weeks or months of design time, development time, and possibly years on the learning curve. You see, it is infinitely easier to reverse-engineer something that is already put together than to try to build it from the ground up. So a user can import a specific layout or design from the demo and then go to the backend of a page and see the content. You can simply paste your content in place of the *lorem ipsum*. (*Lorem ipsum* is simply fill-in dummy text, based on Latin, that is used in desktop publishing — like website building — to show where the real text would go, and it is widely used in the demo content.)

For even greater understanding and an easier reverse-engineering process, you will want to be sure to use a plugin called "Visual Composer" by wpbakery, which we will dive into in detail in the next chapter.

Different themes have different ways of importing content, so be sure to refer to the documentation that comes with the theme to explain how to add demo content. In most cases it is as simple as going to a designated dashboard on the backend and selecting which version of the demo you want to import, then pressing the "Import " button. Or it may require you to navigate to the theme bundle you downloaded and upload a physical file. In either case it is rather simple to do; just be sure to stick to the documentation. If you have any questions, this is when you refer to the comments section of the theme author's page. Many times people have the same question, so to save time, be sure to scan through the last three to four pages of comments for a quick answer rather than waiting a day or two for the developer's reply.

Visual Composer

This plugin is another groundbreaking tool for the novice user. As the name implies, it offers a visual representation of the content inside the editor. For example, if I have a page on the frontend of the website that has a large banner image and some copy split up into two columns, I can easily find and replace that information on the backend editor because the content will match the layout of the content on the frontend — as opposed to a block of text that requires me to read through and replace my web copy with the demo copy in between lines of code. The great news is that many themes will already use Visual Composer and it will be included with the theme in your downloaded content.

Keep in mind Visual Composer is a third-party plugin, meaning the theme developer did not create Visual

Composer but rather offers a version with the purchase of the theme, with the permission of wpbakery. You will still need to purchase a license for Visual Composer if you want to update it (which you will need to do).

Some themes do not offer Visual Composer with the theme, yet they are compatible. Just be sure to read the details for compatibility, which are found on the bottom right of the page in themeforest.net when you are on a theme page.

Finally, there are tons of themes out there that do not use Visual Composer but have their own visual builder. This is perfectly fine. The only reason I advocate for Visual Composer is that it is extremely well documented, with tons of videos and tutorials from the development company wpbakery. Some of the other visual builders are very good — in fact, I prefer some others over Visual Composer. But for the novice user, VIsual Composer is the easiest to start and offers well- documented, robust tools that will ultimately get you to your goal— a high-quality, business-ready

website — more efficiently, so it is my top pick for you.

Must-Haves

This section is about the minimum number of tools that I

recommend you start with. While not exhaustive or absolute,

they are important tools that I value for my own clients'

education and longevity.

cPanel Hosting with a Wordpress Install Script: If you are not sure if your hosting company offers this, be sure to call and ask them directly. This should be a free tool they offer inside cPanel and NOT an add-on or service. Do not use a "Wordpress" hosting package — it is limiting and offers fewer tools than cPanel.

Premium theme: Purchase your theme from a reputable theme market and do a bit of homework on its developer. Make sure it is responsive to customer care issues, and look for a high rating/review from other customers.

Premium theme requirements: This is two-fold and boils down to the features below:

> **Visual Composer Plugin:** I am only recommending one plugin as a must-have for everyone, regardless of industry or niche. Make sure that the premium theme you purchase is compatible with Visual Composer and/or offers it with the theme.

Demo Content: Be sure that the premium theme offers demo content installers.

There are literally thousands of plugins available for nearly every need imaginable, and I can recommend two or three must-haves off the top of my head *depending on your needs*. Because plugins are so very specific, I will not go into the various plugins for each niche, but if you are looking for recommendations for a plugin solution, feel free to email me directly at "shane@integritywebstudios.com" and I would be happy to help you.

Suggested Plugins

When it comes to plugins, premium is not always better. Unlike my preachings about using only premium themes, that is not the case with plugins. Many times the free plugin will work just fine. Granted, almost all of them will have an upgrade available, but I can *usually* find a plugin to do the trick for free. This is because you often need a plugin for a very specific task without a lot of bells and whistles. When searching for free plugins, I always suggest trying the plugins that are most popular, but don't settle for a plugin just because it is most popular. Many times a plugin will just miss the mark in what you are looking for. I would suggest that if you try one and it does not do **everything** that you want it to, simply delete it and try another. Many times I find there is the exact solution I need in a simple, free plugin, but it may take me four or five different plugin tests before I find the perfect one.

To get an idea of some of the amazing capabilities that plugins can add to your Wordpress website, I highly recommend taking an hour to shop for premium plugins. You can view them in themeforest.net by navigating to the "Wordpress" tab and hovering over it to reveal a dropdown of theme categories. At the very bottom of the theme categories dropdown you will see a link to "Wordpress Plugins." This is not about simply window shopping but about getting an idea of what awesome stuff is out there.

I still do this often. Browsing through the various new premium plugins not only shows me great tools for solutions I have had trouble with in the past, but it often sparks ideas for my clients or even my personal businesses. Most premium plugins cost between $15 and $35, but some plugins require a subscription to a service of some kind. For example, the MLS data-feed plugin requires a monthly subscription fee of around $50 or so and a current Realtor's license.

Plugin Overload

As awesome as plugins are, they also have a major flaw. Plugins come at a price (free or not). The price is that plugins can be a drain on your hosting resources (remember we discussed resources in cPanel). Plugins vary greatly, and different plugins can pull more resources than others, so the general rule of thumb is this: If the plugin will not add value to your website for your users, then you do not need it. If you can run a professional website without any plugins, then go for it. On the other hand, if you absolutely need five plugins to make your site a valuable tool/resource for your user, then do it — just be as minimal as possible with plugins when you can.

Quick Summary

We have learned how to setup Wordpress from the ground up using tools that are easily available to expedite your build.

We chose a reputable hosting company that is within budget to purchase a hosting package with cPanel. We set up a free email account inside cPanel and used a cPanel install script to setup Wordpress. For those without the install script, we learned how to manually install Wordpress from the ground up. Once we set up our Wordpress framework, we shopped for a theme from themeforest.net and picked a theme that had the minimum requirements: provide demo content, use Visual Composer, and is a reputable developer/development company that has a star rating and quick turnaround on answering questions about bugs and other issues. We learned how to create a page inside our Wordpress website and now understand the difference between a post and a page. We have explored the vast number of tools available via the use of plugins, but we understand that they are taxing to our new business website so we must limit their use in general.

Designing Tips

As a novice Wordpress developer, stick closely to a theme's layout, at least early on in your Wordpress experience. Though the Visual Composer plugin and other visual editors make it very easy to create fascinating layouts, I suggest staying close to the layout of the demo you chose. We absolutely want to change every image and must add our original copy, but keeping it in the same layout overall will help newbies adhere to better web practices in general. Not that all themes actually stick to the best web practices, but generally they will get you closer than you likely would achieve on your own unless you have some web and/or design experience.

One way you can test the validity of high-quality web practices for layout and design on a theme or demo you are considering is to look at some really well-funded companies that have great user experiences. For example, Home Depot, Best Buy and Blinds.com are a few that come to mind. Companies like these have a huge amount of resources that test every aspect of their websites and meticulously track changes so every button, word and photo placement is well thought out and tested for a high-quality user experience.

Not For You

Most important, design for your customers, **not** yourself. I often struggle with this myself. Before I submit any custom designs to a client for review, I check to make sure that what I have created is aligned with the client's customer/user. If I find that it does not align, I always scratch the whole thing and start over. This has cost me countless hours of work, but it has earned my clients countless dollars. Remember, the reason you are designing a website is not to claim a flashy piece of the web, but to inform, educate, and nurture new customers or clients.

Maintenance

As discussed earlier, Wordpress is constantly upgrading its framework, and it is not uncommon to have a few updates in a week. The same also applies to the plugins that you have on your website. As the Wordpress framework updates, the plugins all have to make updates to stay functional with Wordpress. As a minimum requirement of owning a Wordpress website, someone must log in and update all the plugins and/or framework at least once a month and back up the website. Once a week is preferable, but once a month is sufficient in most cases.

Keep in mind that when an update is released, it could be a security patch for a newly discovered vulnerability or hack, not just another cool feature. The number one reason for hacked websites is outdated versions. Wordpress is very safe as long as you keep it updated properly. The good news is that Wordpress has made it a snap to update anything from inside the CMS.

Updating Wordpress

To begin you will need to be on the backend already logged in to the CMS. When you are on your main dashboard inside the CMS, you will see a red circle with a number in it in one or two places. The first is next to the "Updates" tab right below the Home tab. The other will be next to plugins. You will only see the red circle if you have updates for either a plugin or the framework, so do not be alarmed if you do not have any. If you have a Wordpress update you will also see a message at the top of every page inside the CMS: "WordPress Version X is available! Please update now." If you click on the update you will be brought to the update page where you will see a message that "An updated version of WordPress is available" along with a reminder message to make sure you backup your database before proceeding with your update. Be sure to make a backup **before** proceeding. You will want to back up weekly (preferable) or monthly (at the absolute minimum), which is why we tell clients to back up before they make any updates to the framework. If you have new framework releases within a few days of each other, there is no need to back up again unless you have added a lot of new content since your last backup. We will discuss how and where to back up in the next chapter.

To proceed, simply click the large blue "Update Now" button. Once you do this, the website will begin to download and install the update just as any other device or computer, except this will be much quicker. Once the install is finished there will be a welcome message and all the information about the latest version you have just upgraded to, including a video. From here I tell clients to navigate to the frontend and test a few pages and functions to ensure that all is working as expected. There are rare cases when the update can conflict with plugins or simply break the site altogether.

Don't panic: There is an easy way to revert back if you do see an issue, which we will discuss in the next chapter. If you do not have any issues (and most do not) then you are done with the update (until the next one).

Updating Plugins

After we have updated our framework (or ensured that we have no updates) we can now begin updating any plugins. Though this can be done inside the "Update" page, I prefer that clients go to the "Plugins" page and update them there. Once on the plugins page, you will see all of your plugins listed. Any plugins requiring an update will be highlighted or have a highlighted message under them. Inside the highlighted message, if you look to the right there will be a textual link that says "Update Now." Simply click the link and the plugin will show a spinner icon to let you know it is working and begin updating the plugin. Be sure to stay on the page until the plugin has finished updating.

Once completed, the plugin will change to the regular color or remove the highlighted text. After you have finished updating a plugin, you will want to test the site again just like we did when we updated our Wordpress framework. If all is well we simply go on to the next plugin and repeat the process (including the testing) until all plugins have been updated. From start to finish all your updates and testing should take you no more than 10 minutes tops. The reason I tell clients to update one by one as opposed to simply selecting them all and updating at once on the "Update" page is that if there was ever an issue, we want to know exactly which plugin caused the problem. By "updating all," it is nearly impossible to tell which plugin caused the issue, which means once the site is fixed we have to test each and every plugin. This can be done by you, but at this point most clients simply have us fix it for them. If we know what plugin caused the issue, then it is an easy fix and the clients are billed for an hour. If the client does not know which plugin caused the problem, it can easily double or even triple the time and become a costly problem. Again, Wordpress is very stable, and this is a rare circumstance, but that little habit can save you big. Now let's talk about preventative maintenance and security.

Backups

If you ever have an issue with a broken website, whether from an issue of upgrading or a hack, your easiest fix will be to revert back to the last stable version. Luckily there is an easy-to-use tool that you already have that can do this. There is a backup tool built into our installer script program we used to install and setup Wordpress in our easy installation section. In order to get to the tool, we need to login to cPanel and navigate to the same installer tool we used to set up. If you do not remember where and how to get there, be sure to jump back to the "Installing Wordpress" chapter under "Easy Installation" for details.

PLEASE NOTE: If you had to do a manual install you will also need to do a manual backup. We will discuss it in the next section. However, we will not discuss how to do a manual restore since this is out of the scope of purpose for this book. Due to its complexity, I recommend that novice Wordpress builders contact the hosting company to help you restore the website manually. Some hosting companies will charge you, while others may simply walk you through it on the phone for free. In either case, having current backups is a **necessity** because without them the site will not be able to be replaced/reverted.

Automated Backups

Once you are inside your installer you will see a section labeled "My Applications" or "Installed Applications." Depending on your hosting company's setup, this is where your quick install details will be found. You may need to click to view the list of installs or applications, or it may be on the page already. Simply look for the name of the website, which is what the system calls the "application." To the right of the application name is a series of icons: simply hover over them to find the "Backup" icon. Once inside you have an option to create backups or restore backups (sometimes restoring will have a separate navigation link in the top of the page, so be sure to look around or call your hosting provider for quick, easy walk-through of how/where to go).

Needless to say, we must have first made a backup in order to have one available to restore it. As mentioned in the previous chapter, I encourage clients to back up both the database and the files before every framework update. Since updates happen at least once a month, it also builds a good backup library. Simply find the last backup you created before your update (it will be dated), select it and click "Restore." Once the process is done, your site will be back to awesome in no time. If your site crashed because of a Wordpress framework update, give it a week before trying again to see if any new updates come out; many times the developer will release updates to patch a problem upgrade if the same issue happens to a lot of people. If nothing new comes out, contact the developer of the premium theme for help. Next, we will talk about security.

Manual Backups

To manually backup your Wordpress website, we will need to back up two different items: the files and the database. To do this we will need to be inside cPanel, so let's go there now.

Manually Backup the Files

Once you are inside cPanel, navigate to your "File Manager" and go to the root of the file stack. You can tell if it is the "root" if you can see a file named "public_html." If you do not see that and only see your Wordpress files (which consist of three folders: wp-admin, wp-content and wp-includes, along with about 15 or so .php files), go to the lowest point in the file stack, the root. You may need to change the settings in the cPanel file manager to see/access the root. Simply click on "Settings," located at the top right of the page. When you click "Settings" it opens a popup preferences panel that states, "Always open this directory in the future by default" and allows you to select which option you like. We need to select "Home Directory," then save. In addition, I also like to select "Show Hidden Files" and "Disable Character Encoding Check." You will now be able to go up one level and see the public_html folder.

Now that you can see the public_html folder, we want to compress it into a zip file for easier/quicker downloading. To do this, right-click on the icon and select "Compress," then choose .zip. I suggest naming the file with the date (for example backup-3-12-16.zip). The system will compress the files and create a new zip file that you can store where it is created or download for a local copy (preferable).

Manually Backup the Database

Now back out of the file manager and into cPanel. Once inside cPanel again, look for the "Databases" section and select the icon that says "phpMyAdmin." This will open up a database manager. Since you only have one website installed, click on the the database name (the only other option is information_schema and that is not it). The database will open up and you will see a list of tables. Above the list select "Export," then choose "Quick" if not already selected, and then select "SQL" for the format. Now click "Go." The system will ask you to name it and download the .sql file to your computer. Congratulations! You have just backed up your database.

Security

It is important not only to keep your website up to date but also recommended to use a third- party security to help protect against other malicious attacks. For as little as $10 a month you can sign on to a security company that can monitor and protect the website. The security is **not** a must-have because if you are backing up the website regularly, a hack would simply be an inconvenience, not a devastation (unless you did not fix it for a long period of time).

So, the first thing to understand about security is that hackers are not looking to hack *your* website but rather attack *any* website. They target large groups of servers as opposed to individuals — but on the bright side, this also makes it easier to protect your website. There is **no guarantee against hacking**. Think of the large, name-brand companies that have been hacked in the last few years — Sony, Home Depot, Target, just to name a few. Please understand these companies were specifically targeted and not just random malicious hacks like we are talking about here.

Though possible, we are fortunate that this is not the type of hack we have to face. We are not targets but rather part of a group that was connected to another group. Also worth remembering is that these third-party securities are your second line of defense in protecting your website. The first line of defense is simply keeping it updated regularly. To demonstrate this, imagine installing the latest home monitoring security network with all the best features to protect your home from burglars. Will that security system prevent a thief from getting in your home if you have a five-foot hole in the brick wall on the side of the house? Probably not: That is the equivalent of using a security plugin and not updating regularly. The updates "patch" (or fix holes in) our natural securities and site structure to eliminate such risks.

There are a lot of good security companies made just for Wordpress, but I have a few that I prefer. This list is not exhaustive, nor am I saying these are the absolute best, but these are the few I use most often and find the most helpful for me and my clients.

Wordfence: Found here: https://www.wordfence.com

Sucuri.net: Found here: https://sucuri.net/

Site Guarding: Found here: https://www.siteguarding.com/en

In Summary

At this point you should have a high-quality website built — or at the very least, a clear understanding of what it takes to build your very own Wordpress website for your business.

We discussed the hosting company, the importance of cPanel, domain email setup, installing Wordpress, choosing a high-quality theme, installing demo content, Visual Composer, design tips, maintenance, backups and security.

Wow! Give yourself a high five, this is a pretty big list of things you now know how to do. I hope you enjoy your new website and more importantly I hope that it delivers a return on investment.

If you have any questions, comments or scenarios that you would like to learn about, please first check my Learning Wordpress video tutorials at www.integritywebstudios.com. If you do not see the answer to your question, then please drop me a line at shane@integritywebstudios.com and I will be happy to help you or even do an entire video tutorial for you.

Notes

Use this section to take notes.

Account Info & Passwords

Save login info such as usernames and passwords for

hosting, cPanel, email and Wordpress.

URL:

UN:

PW:

Other:

Notes:

URL:

UN:

PW:

Other:

Notes:

URL:

UN:

PW:

Other:

Notes:

URL:

UN:

PW:

Other:

Notes:

URL:

UN:

PW:

Other:

Notes:

URL:

UN:

PW:

Other:

Notes:

URL:

UN:

PW:

Other:

Notes:

URL:

UN:

PW:

Other:

Notes:

URL:

UN:

PW:

Other:

Notes:
